Contents

Four seasons

The weather is different all over the world. And it changes everywhere at different times of the year. But most places have a particular kind of weather at certain times. We call these times seasons.

In springtime, woods and meadows are full of colourful flowers.

Summer days are long and warm.

In autumn it's time to clear up all the leaves that have fallen from the trees.

There are four seasons – **spring**, summer, **autumn** and winter. In summer it is usually warm and dry, but in winter it is cold and wet. Spring and autumn have weather that is somewhere in between.

In winter, playing in the snow can be lots of fun.

Why are there seasons?

Planet **Earth** is constantly travelling through space, circling our very own star, the sun. The hot sun gives us our light, heat and energy. It takes a year for Earth to travel around the sun.

The Earth **tilts** slightly to one side as it travels around the sun.

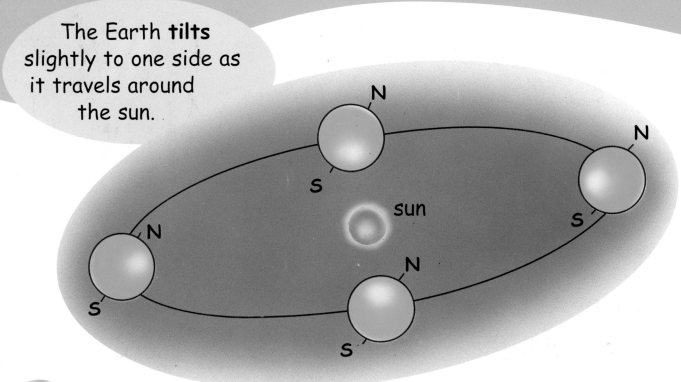

N

S

N

S

sun

N

S

N

S

In summer we get most direct light and warmth from the sun.

As the year passes, different parts of Earth turn more directly towards the sun. Then they turn away again and get less direct sunlight. This is what causes our seasons.

Spring is here

In spring many trees are covered in masses of tiny flowers called blossom.

Spring is the season between winter and summer. Everyone looks forward to springtime. This is when the days start to get longer and the sun climbs higher in the sky each day.

Lambs eat juicy grass to help them grow.

In spring, birds build their nests and lay eggs, and sheep give birth to their lambs. The warmer days make plants start to grow, and trees suddenly burst into bud. Before long they are covered in colourful **blossom**.

Birds often build their nests in trees and hedges.

It's summertime!

Summer is the hottest part of the year. This is because the sun is higher in the sky and shines down more directly.

It's fun to play by the sea when the weather is hot.

As well as being hot, summer days are longest. At the height of summer it stays light for longer than any other time of year, and the mild nights are very short.

A warm sea breeze is good for flying kites.

Autumn leaves

The autumn season follows summer. The weather starts getting cooler and wetter again, and the days get shorter.

In autumn, you will often see frost in the mornings.

Squirrels are always very busy in autumn collecting nuts. They bury some of them to eat next year.

Autumn leaves make this a very colourful season.

The leaves on many trees lose their green colour and turn yellow, orange and even bright red. Then they drop to the ground, which is why in America this season is called the '**fall**'.

Cold winter

Winter is the coldest time of year. The sun stays low in the sky all day, so that even on a fine day it is not very warm. The shortest day of the year is right in the middle of winter.

Outdoor skating is fun on a cold, bright day.

The trees are wrapped in a blanket of snow.

The dormouse rolls up into a ball for its winter sleep.

Many parts of the world have snow in wintertime. Snow, **ice** and cold days make it difficult for animals to find food, so some of them **hibernate** and sleep through until spring.

The farming year

Farmers follow the changing weather of the seasons. In spring they **plough** their fields before planting the seeds that will grow into crops. Lambs and many other baby animals are born in springtime.

Before summer, farmers **shear** sheep for their wool.

This tractor is pulling a machine to sow seeds.

A combine harvester cuts the ripe wheat and separates the grain all at once.

Crops may need extra water in summer, and by autumn they are ready to be **harvested**. This is a very busy time for farmers. Then in winter they plan and prepare for next spring.

Upside-down seasons

When the top half of the world – called the **northern hemisphere** – is tilted towards the sun, it is summer there. At the same time the bottom half, or **southern hemisphere**, is tilted away. So there it is winter.

In the northern hemisphere it's cold in December.

18

Father Christmas gets very hot in Australia. There it's mid-summer at the end of the year.

When it is cold and wintry in Europe or North America, it is warm and summery in Australia or South America.

In the tropics

The tropics are a broad area around the **equator**. In this **tropical zone** there are two main seasons. One is hot and wet, and the other is slightly cooler and often dry.

These trees and plants are growing in an oasis. This is an area in a desert where there is a spring or well of water.

The world's **rainforests** lie in the tropics. Here the seasons hardly change all year, and the warm wet conditions make a perfect home for many kinds of life.

Half of the world's animals and plants live and grow in the rainforests.

Land of the midnight sun

At the North and South Poles
the weather is cold all year round. The
main difference between the seasons
is the amount of daylight. It is light
all summer long, and dark all winter.

It's hard
to see the
Arctic fox
against
the snow.

Emperor penguins huddle together in the bitterly cold Antarctic winter.

For this reason the region around the **North Pole**, called the **Arctic**, is also known as 'the land of the midnight sun'. At the North Pole, the sun rises at the beginning of summer and sets six months later.

Following the seasons

Animals and people live by the seasons, and some travel great distances as the weather changes. The Sami people, or Lapps, of northern **Scandinavia** live a traditional life herding reindeer.

In winter the Sami follow their herds south to warmer pastures.

Every year grey whales swim down from Alaska to warmer waters off Mexico.

Many birds and animals **migrate** as winter comes near. Most lay their eggs or give birth to their young in spring, so that the youngsters can grow up in warm weather.

Swallows meet up in groups before flying south for the winter.

Celebrating the changing year

It's been a good harvest.

A summer fiesta, or holiday, in Spain.

In ancient times, people thanked the gods on special days for the coming of spring and the middle of summer. All over the world, festivals are still held to celebrate important seasonal events.

Elephants parade through the streets in this Buddhist festival in Sri Lanka.

Harvest festival is one of the most important celebrations. People give thanks for a good harvest with gifts and decorations of fruit, vegetables and **sheaves** of yellow corn. The summer is over, but it will not be long before another new spring arrives.

Do it yourself

You can keep a record
of the changing seasons.

Make your own nature diary

1 Draw a simple map of your garden.
If you don't have your own garden, you
could ask to draw a map of a friend's or
relative's, or perhaps the school garden.

2 Divide the garden map into squares,
numbered A to E down one side and 1 to 5
across the top. Each square has its own
name (for example, the top-left square is A1).

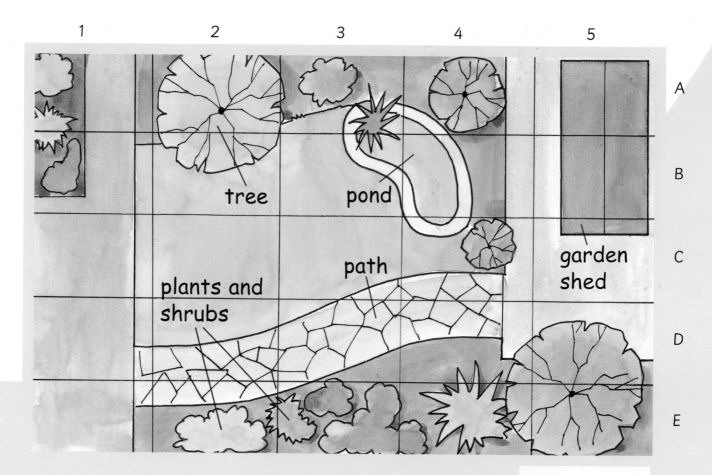

3 Keep a diary of what you see in each square every day or once a week – the trees, flowers, birds or animal tracks and anything else you notice. You could also make a note of the weather.

See how the seasons change!

This is how your garden map might look.

Glossary

Arctic The cold region around the North Pole.

autumn The season between summer and winter, when many trees lose their leaves.

blossom A mass of small flowers that appear on trees.

crops Plants that are grown by farmers as food, such as cereals and vegetables.

Earth The planet on which we live.

equator An imaginary circle around the middle of the Earth.

fall An American word for autumn.

harvested The gathering in of ripened crops.

hibernate To spend the winter asleep.

ice Frozen water.

migrate To travel from one region to another.

North Pole The point at the very top of the Earth, in the middle of the frozen Arctic Ocean.

northern hemisphere The top half of the Earth, above the equator.

plough To break up and turn over the soil and earth.

rainforests Thick forests found in warm, wet tropical areas.

Scandinavia A cold region in northern Europe, including Norway and Sweden.

shear Sheep used to have their wool cut with big scissors called shears. We still say they have been sheared, even though today electric clippers are used.

sheaves Bundles of corn-stalks, tied together.

southern hemisphere The bottom half of the Earth, below the equator.

spring The season between winter and summer, when days start to get warmer.

tilts Slants or leans slightly to one side.

tropical zone A very hot region close to the equator.

index

2010?

Our World

Seasons

Neil Morris

Chrysalis Children's Books

First published in the UK in 2002 by
Chrysalis Children's Books
An imprint of Chrysalis Books Group Plc
The Chrysalis Building, Bramley Road
London W10 6SP

Paperback edition first published in 2005

ISBN 1 84138 415 1 (hb)
ISBN 1 84458 236 1 (pb)

British Library Cataloguing in Publication Data
for this book is available from the British Library.

Series editor: Jean Coppendale
Designer: Peter Clayman
Artwork: Chris Forsey
Picture researchers: Terry Forshaw and Jenny Barlow
Consultant: Bethan Currenti

Printed in China

10 9 8 7 6 5 4 3 2 1

Picture acknowledgements:

(T) = Top, (B) = Bottom, (L) = Left, (R) = Right.

B = Bubbles, C = Corbis, CO = Collections, DV = Digital Vision,
FLPA = Frank Lane Picture Agency, GI = Getty Images, P = Papilio,
SP = Still Pictures, SPL = Science Photo Library.

Front cover & 14 (B) Wayne W. Lockwood/C; title page , 7 & back cover (L) DV; 4 & front cover
(insets) Ecoscene/C; 5 (T) DV, (B) Julie Habel/C; 8 (T) Darrell Gulin/C, (B) & back cover (R) Carl &
Ann Purcell/C; 9 Julie Habel/C; 10 Angela Hampton/B; 11 DV; 12 (L) Yann Arthus-Bertrand/C, (R)
Vaughan Fleming/SPL; 13 Jamie Harron/P; 14 (T) Bob Winsett/C; 15 & front cover (inset) George
McCarthy/C; 16 (T) Dewitt Jones/C, (B) Richard Hamilton Smith/C; 17 Ecoscene/C; 18 & 31
(TL) Gill Jones/CO; 19 Douglas Peebles/C; 20 Wolfgang Kaehler/C; 21 Roland Seitre/SP; 22 &
front cover (inset) Kennan Ward/C; 23 & 31 (R) Kim Westerskov/GI; 24 Bryan & Cherry
Alexander; 25 (T) Norbert Wu/SP, (B) P.Heard/FLPA; 26 (L) K.M. Westermann/C, (R) Brian
Shuel/CO; 27 Adam Woolfitt/C.

THE AZTECS

by Robert Nicholson and Claire Watts

Editorial Consultant: Penny Bateman,
Education Department, British Museum

TWO-CAN

First published in Great Britain in 1991 by
Two-Can Publishing Ltd
346 Old Street
London EC1V 9NQ

Printed and bound in Hong Kong

This impression published 1991 in association with Scholastic
Publications Ltd.

4 6 8 10 9 7 5 3

British Library Cataloguing in Publication Data
Nicholson, Robert
    The Aztecs
    1. Mexico, Aztecs, history
    I. Title II. Watts, Claire
    972.004974

ISBN: 1-85434-052-2

Photographic credits:
Werner Forman: p.8, p.9, p.10, p.11, p.12, p.14, p.15, p.16(c), p.17, p.18, p.20, p.21, p.22(t),
p.22(c), p.22(b), p.30(c); Ronald Sheridan: p.8, p.13, p.30(t); Toby Maudsley: p.15(b), p.16(t)

Illustration credits:
Harry Clow: p.6, p.7, p.9, p.11, p.13, p.14, p.16, p.17, p.18, p.19, p.20, p.23, p.24; Jon Davis/
Linden Artists: p.4, p.5; Maxine Hamil: Cover, pp 25-29

Contents

All words in **bold** can be found in the glossary

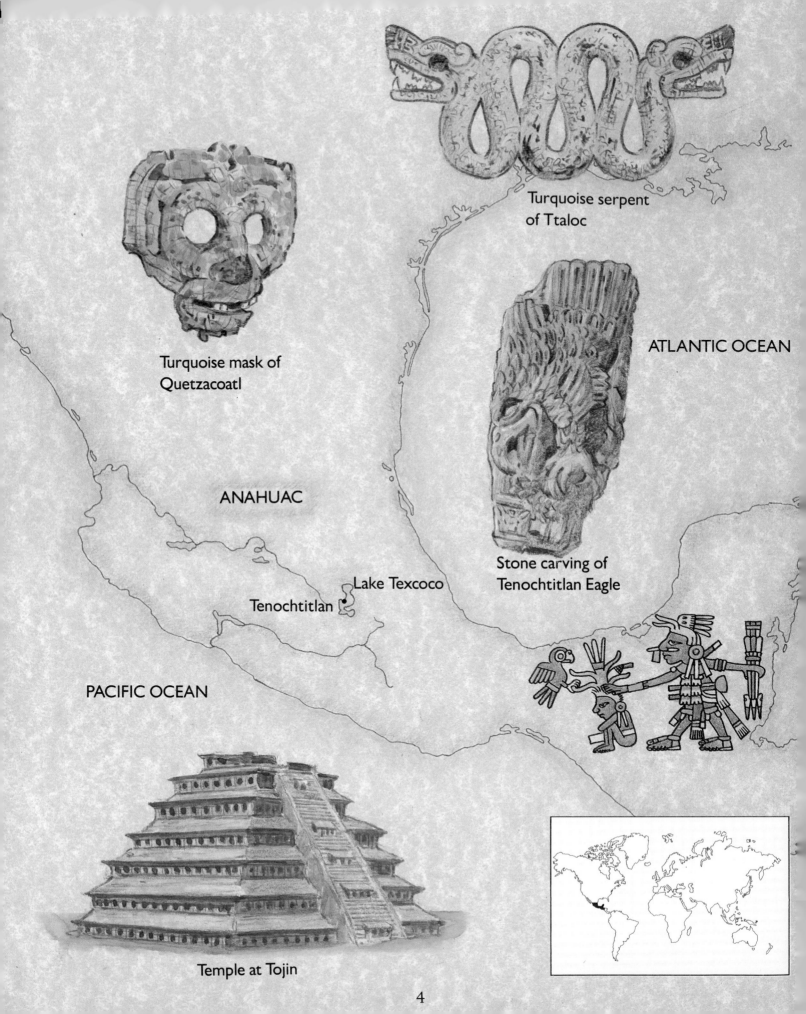

Turquoise serpent
of Ttaloc

Turquoise mask of
Quetzacoatl

ATLANTIC OCEAN

ANAHUAC

Lake Texcoco

Tenochtitlan

Stone carving of
Tenochtitlan Eagle

PACIFIC OCEAN

Temple at Tojin

4

The Aztec World

Over 500 years ago a powerful people called the Aztecs lived in the region we now call Mexico. They defeated all the other peoples who lived in this area. The Aztecs built a huge city called Tenochtitlan, as large as any city in Europe at the time. They called their land **Anahuac**, which means *the land on the edge of the waters*. Many of the Aztecs were fearless warriors who set out to capture people to **sacrifice** to please their gods. They also fought the people who lived around them, stole their crops and livestock and carried them off to use as slaves.

Aztec Lands

Anahuac was divided across the middle by high mountains. The Aztecs built their city, Tenochtitlan, on a **plateau** high in the mountains. Other smaller villages were built there too.

In the lower land on each side lay thick, steamy, tropical rainforest. This region was uncomfortable to live in and the land was not very good for farming, although some people lived there.

The weather in Anahuac followed a very regular pattern. At the beginning of the year, there was a dry growing season, then a hot, wet summer from May to October, followed by a short, cold winter.

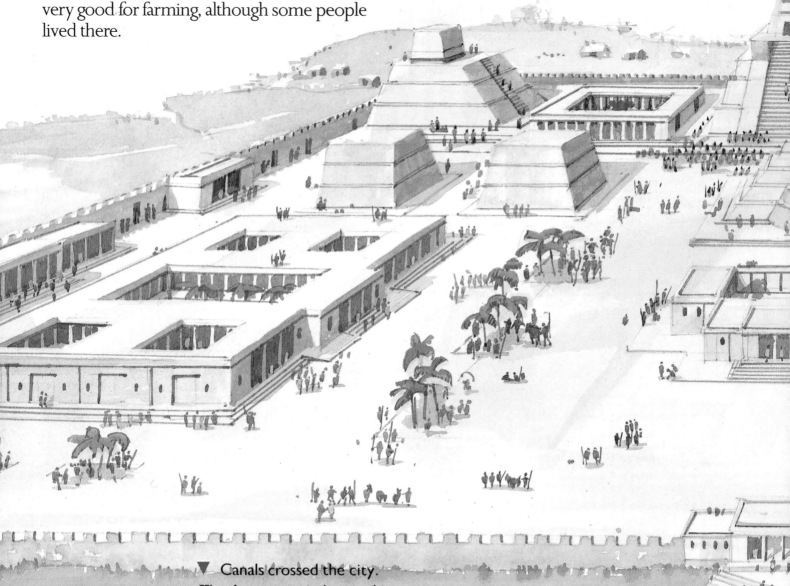

▼ Canals crossed the city. The Aztecs carried everything by water or on their backs. They did not use vehicles with wheels at all.

▼ The main temple dominated the city. It was over 50m tall.

▼ Tenochtitlan was built on a big island in the middle of a lake.

◄ There were three main **causeways** built to reach the island. They were made of volcanic rock and earth and were joined to the island and the land by bridges that could be knocked aside if enemies were about to enter the city.

The Great Speakers

The Aztecs were divided into small family groups called **calpollis**. Each had a head man who represented the group whenever decisions had to be made.

The head men of the calpollis of noble families made up a council who elected a ruler called the Huey Hatoanni, which means **great speaker**. He was a nobleman who had been trained as a priest, but he also had to be a brave warrior because fighting was such an important part of Aztec life.

The Great Speaker also led his people to war. The Aztecs were constantly at war with neighbouring peoples. They fought battles to capture people rather than kill them, in order to provide victims to sacrifice to their gods.

▶ Montezuma wore this huge and elaborate feather head-dress at ceremonies and processions.

▼ This carved stone box contained the ashes of one of the Great Speakers.

Some Important Leaders

ITZCOATL was the first great leader of the Aztecs. He became Great Speaker in 1426. He spread Aztec power far beyond Tenochtitlan. He also built new temples and causeways in the city.

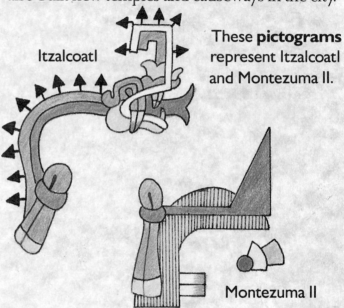

Itzalcoatl

These **pictograms** represent Itzalcoatl and Montezuma II.

Montezuma II

MONTEZUMA II became Great Speaker in 1502 and made the empire bigger than it had ever been before. Unfortunately, the Aztecs were soon to be defeated by the Spanish (*see page 24*).

Aztec Gods

Religion affected every part of Aztec life. There were hundreds of gods, and each one represented a different part of the natural world or human activity. The Aztecs believed very strongly that the gods had decided what would happen to each person before he or she was born. They also believed that the priests could foretell events in the future.

The other peoples in Mexico believed in many of the same gods as the Aztecs. All these gods were linked by a complicated set of myths and histories.

The Aztecs had two calendars. In the religious calendar the year had only 260 days, but the solar calendar had 365 days, like ours. Their solar year was divided into 18 months, each with 20 days, and 5 extra days.

The Fifth Sun

The Aztecs believed that the world had lived through the destruction of four suns before the coming of the present, fifth sun. The first sun had been destroyed by jaguars, the second by hurricanes, the third by fire and the fourth by floods. The fifth was to be destroyed by earthquakes.

▶ The Aztec calendar stone shows the sun god surrounded by symbols of the final earthquake. Around this are the days of the Aztec year.

◀ This stone statue is Coatlicue, the goddess of the Earth.

Important Gods

HUITZILOPOCHTLI was the patron god of the Aztecs. His name means *blue hummingbird*. He was the god of war. The Aztecs fought a special war every year called *the war of the flowers* in order to capture victims to sacrifice to Huitzilopochtli.

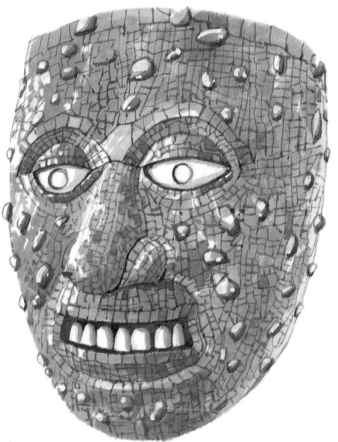

▲Quetzalcoatl was shown with a much friendlier face than many of the other gods.

QUETZALCOATL was the god of learning, hope and healing. His name means *feathered serpent*. The original Quetzalcoatl was probably a king of the Toltec tribe who ruled Mexico long before the Aztecs. According to legend, one day Quetzalcoatl would appear to decide the fate of the Aztecs.

Aztec Temples

The Aztecs built large four-sided **pyramids** for their gods. At the top of each pyramid was the temple where ceremonies took place and sacrifices were made.

Near many temples there was a sort of basketball court for playing a ceremonial game with a hard rubber ball. Players had to move the ball using only their hips and knees.

Priests were highly thought of by the Aztec people but they led a very hard life. They had to fast regularly and were not allowed to cut or wash their hair. Their hair usually stood out all around their heads, covered in insects. Priests and the women helpers in the temple were not allowed to marry. The priests studied the stars and foretold future events. Only the priests would dare venture out after dark, as the spirits of the dark, which were believed to steal people's souls, were thought to have no power over priests.

◀ Many steps led up to the temple on top of a pyramid.

▼ A heavy, sharp stone knife like this would be used to cut out the victim's heart. The heart was then burnt on a fire in the temple.

Sacrifices

Human sacrifices were the most important part of Aztec religion. The Aztecs believed that the heart and blood of victims kept their gods strong and powerful, so that they would protect the people and make their crops grow. They also thought that when they sacrificed a brave soldier his strength would pass to their warriors.

Most victims were captured enemy soldiers, but at some ceremonies Aztec men, women and children were sacrificed. The biggest sacrifice was in the reign of Montezuma II when 12,000 enemy soldiers were sacrificed at once.

Every morning each person would make a small sacrifice by pricking their finger or ear lobe with a cactus needle and letting a drop of blood fall and soak into the ground.

Farming

Many Aztecs, even those who lived in or around the main cities, were farmers. Each farmer gave the Great Speaker a little of his crops which would be stored until the people needed extra food in times of famine.

Corn was the most important crop grown, but the Aztecs also grew **squash**, avocados, beans, sweet potatoes, peppers and tomatoes.

Farmland

Aztec tools were very simple. There were no ploughs and the main tool was a small **digging stick**. The Aztecs used it to dig trenches to plant seeds in.

There were two types of farmland. Some Aztec farmers cleared a small part of the land or forest by burning down the vegetation. They would then plant crops in the fertile ashes. After a few years, when the land became less fertile, they would move on to burn another area.

Around Tenochtitlan, the Aztecs dug up fertile mud from the lake bottom and heaped it on top of woven plant material to make little islands. On these they planted their crops. The islands were called **chinampas** or *floating gardens*.

▶ Sometimes trees were planted to anchor the chinampas to the lake bottom.

Aztec Crops

PEPPER

AVOCADO

TOMATO

CORN

SWEET POTATO

Food

The Aztecs ate a lot of different vegetables, but scarcely any meat. There were few large wild animals to hunt in Anahuac, and the Aztecs kept no cattle or sheep. The vegetables they ate, such as corn and beans, were full of protein so this made up for the lack of meat. A sort of corn pancake, called a **tlaxcalli**, was eaten with most meals.

Food Facts

● Only rich Aztecs could afford to drink chocolate, as cacao beans, which chocolate is made from, were also used as money!

● A very strong drink called **pulque** was made out of a sort of cactus.

● At religious ceremonies special little cakes were made in the shapes of the gods.

● The Aztecs bred chickens, turkeys and even dogs to eat, and also caught fish and wild rabbits.

◀ The Aztecs ate from pottery bowls like this one, using their fingers.

Make your own Tlaxcallis

Ingredients

450 g plain flour
1 tsp baking powder
1 tsp salt
1½ tbsp margarine
175 ml cold water

1. Mix the dry ingredients together. Rub in the margarine until the mixture resembles bread-crumbs.

2. Add the water gradually and stir in with a wooden spoon until the mixture forms a stiff dough.

3. Divide the dough into 12 balls. On a floured surface, roll the balls out into thin circles.

4. Ask a grown-up to help you to melt a little fat in a frying pan and fry the tlaxcallis for 1 minute each side.

Serve your tlaxcallis warm. Use them to make parcels filled with chilli, avocado, chopped tomato and lettuce.

17

At Home

Poor Aztecs lived in small, one-roomed houses, which were made from branches plastered with mud. The roofs were thatched.

Town houses, owned by more wealthy people, were usually bigger. They were often built on raised platforms and had walls made of volcanic stone, which is easy to carve and shape. The walls were then covered with cement made from limestone, which made the outside of the house white and shiny. Several rooms opened on to an internal courtyard.

Instead of a bathroom, many houses had a separate sweat-room. These were built from stone, which could be heated by building fires around the outside walls. Inside, the Aztecs would splash water on to the hot walls to make them steam. A person would stay inside until he began to sweat and then dash out and plunge into the nearest stream or pool.

▼ A statue of Xiuhtectuhtli was placed in the hearth of each house.

Furniture

The Aztecs had little furniture. They slept on mats in the corners of the room and sat on straw cushions during the day. The focus of the room was the fireplace, where all the cooking was done. It was also used as a shrine to Xiuhtectuhtli.

18

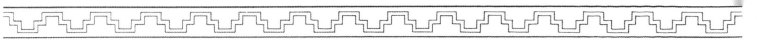

Codices

Aztec children were taught mostly at home by their parents. All boys had to go to a school run by their calpolli where they learnt how to be warriors. Girls did not have to go to school. There were also temple schools where boys of noble families could learn the duties of a priest and girls could learn to be temple assistants or healers.

Writing

The Aztecs did not use letters to write as we do. Instead they used pictograms, which use pictures to represent a word. Several could be joined together to make a sentence. This form of writing was very simple and was mainly used for records, although some history books and religious books were written. Aztec books, or **codices**, were written on folded deerskin or bark paper.

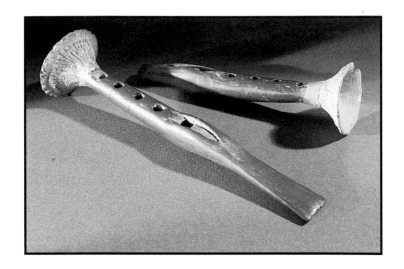

▲ Many children would have learnt to play small flutes like this.

▶ This codex shows offerings made to the sun god at the top and to the god of darkness at the bottom.

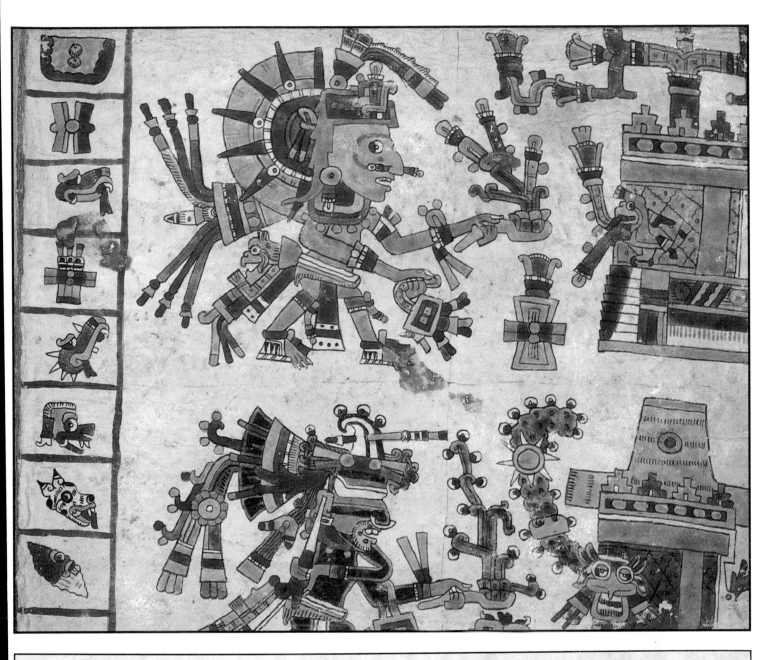

Some Common Pictograms

Like handwriting, pictograms varied depending on the person who drew them. Can you spot any of these in the codex above?

 alligator

 snake

 death

 monkey

 jaguar

 movement

 flint knife

 reed

 rabbit

 eagle

 deer

 vulture

Craft

As the Aztecs did not use money, a person's wealth was judged by the beauty of his possessions. A rich man could afford to have a skilled craftsman make the things he needed. Craftsmen were paid in food or other goods.

Metal

The Aztecs did not use metal for tools or weapons. They did not have iron or any other very strong metal. They used gold and copper to make delicate statues.

▼ This golden ornament was worn through the lip.

Pottery

The Aztecs made fine pots, decorated in gold and black. These were made by building up coils of clay and then smoothing them out, as they did not have pottery wheels.

Stone

The volcanic rock found all over Mexico is quite soft so it could be carved with the stone tools used by the Aztecs. The people made detailed stone carvings and statues from it.

Featherwork

Brightly coloured feathers were trimmed and bound together to make extraordinary collages. These were used to decorate soldiers' shields and head-dresses.

▼ This featherwork disc shows the symbol of a whirlpool.

Obsidian

Volcanic glass called **obsidian** was used to make blades for knives. It was also made into vases and mirrors.

▼ This mirror is made from polished obsidian.

Clothes

Aztec clothes were usually made from fibre from the **maguey plant**. Only the rich could afford cotton. Their garments were often brightly coloured and beautifully embroidered. An Aztec's clothes reflected his age and position in society. Ordinary tribesmen wore a simple loincloth called a **maxtli** and a cape over one shoulder. The head man of a calpolli had a brighter cape. Warriors wore ornate feather head-dresses, and some wore costumes made to look like jaguars or eagles. The Great Speaker wore golden sandals.

Women wore a skirt wrapped around their waists and tied with a belt. On top they wore a loose sleeveless tunic. Most plaited their hair. Both men and women wore jewellery made from jade, emerald and opal. They also wore a lot of bright make-up, yellow and red for the women and black, white and blue for the men.

The Coming of the Spanish

When Montezuma II was Great Speaker, Aztec civilisation reached its peak. Far away in Europe, however, the **Spanish Empire** was looking for new lands to conquer. In 1519, Cortés, the Spanish governor of Cuba, arrived in Mexico with just 400 soldiers.

At first the Aztecs believed that Cortés was the god Quetzalcoatl, come to decide their fate as had been foretold. They did not know whether to welcome him or be wary of him. Within two years the Spanish had defeated the Aztecs, killed most of their population and completely destroyed their main city. The Aztecs had no weapons which could withstand the guns, armour and horses of the Spanish.

▼ Aztec legend said that when the god Quetzalcoatl returned, he would have a pale face, a dark beard and dark legs. To the Aztecs, Cortés with his heavy beard and black leggings even looked like the returning god.

Quetzalcoatl Gives Food to the People

The Aztecs told many stories about their gods and about the world around them. Often these stories would try to explain something that the people did not really understand. This is the story of the discovery of corn.

When the time came for the gods to create people, they found it very difficult. It was much harder than creating the rest of the world. They had made many attempts at making people, all of which came to nothing. Finally they came up with creatures that seemed to be just about right. There was one problem though. The people that they had created did not know how or what to eat. They were starving, but they could not work out what was wrong with them, or what to do about it. The gods did not know how to help the new people. All the other animals that they had created had just started to eat whatever suited them with no help at all from the gods. In fact, the gods themselves did not know what the new people should eat.

Every day the gods sat around, trying to work out how to help the new people. As they watched the people grow thinner and thinner,

the gods began to worry. If these people died out, they would have to start all over again.

One day, the ants came to the place where the gods sat yet again discussing what to do about the starving people.

"We know where there is food," said one of the ants. "We will carry it here for you to give to the new people."

"Wonderful," said the god Quetzalcoatl, who was more worried about the people than any of the other gods. "But why don't you just tell us where the food is, and we will tell the people?"

"No, no, no!" said the ants. "We can't possibly do that. It's a secret."

The ants did not want the people to die. They had a feeling that people might be useful to them

in the future. But they were also rather worried about their own size. They thought that they might be overlooked since they were so tiny and so they wanted to make sure that they were important to the gods. It seemed to them that the best idea was to keep the people alive. In that way they would make sure that the gods needed them.

So, the next day, the ants carried food to the gods. This food was very hard and the pieces of it were so tiny that each of the ants could carry one grain easily. The gods had never seen anything like it. They chewed the hard grains until they were soft and then placed them on the lips of the people. The people swallowed the grains and felt better.

Again and again the ants did this, but they would not tell the gods where the food came from. Every day, the gods had to wait for the ants to bring the grains, then chew it for the people and place it on their lips.

But Quetzalcoatl knew it would not last. Much as he loved the people, he was tired of feeding them. They were his responsibility. All the other gods had different jobs, so while they were chewing food for the people that they had created, they could not make the Sun shine or the rain fall or the rivers flow. Each day, when the ants arrived with the grains, the gods sighed deeply, and grew more irritated.

Once again Quetzalcoatl asked the ants to tell him where the food came from, but they refused. Their secret was much too valuable. So Quetzalcoatl decided to find out for himself.

He turned himself into a black ant and sat waiting at a place that he knew the ants passed every day. As the line of ants marched past, he slipped into the line and marched with them. The procession headed straight towards a huge mountain and into a crack in the side. In a huge cavern Quetzalcoatl saw heaps of food.

Quetzalcoatl realised that there was nothing he could do immediately. Copying the other ants, he picked up a grain and stepped into line.

When the ants reached the place where the other gods were, Quetzalcoatl turned back into his own form.

"You thought yourselves very clever to keep the secret of the grain, but I have been cleverer still!" he said to the ants.

"You may know where the corn is, but you cannot give it to the people without our help.

The people are much too big to fit in through the tiny crack in the mountain that we squeeze through," said one of the ants, and all the other ants nodded.

Quetzalcoatl looked down at the ants and gave a withering smile. He turned to the thunder god, and whispered in his ear.

The thunder god stood up and raised his hand. A flash of lightning came from the clouds and struck the mountain where the food was hidden. A huge crack appeared in the mountain and the grains of corn spilled out.

When the people saw the mountain split they ran to see what had happened. One of them picked up one of the grains and put it in his mouth. He chewed, swallowed and picked up another grain. Gradually the other people began to copy him.

The people ate their fill of the food, but there were many grains left over. Quetzalcoatl showed them how to plant the grains, so that more food would grow. These first plants had only two seeds on them, but, as time passed, they grew and grew until today each plant has many grains. We now call these plants corn.

So, the gods were happy because the people could now fend for themselves. The people were happy because they realised what had been wrong with them and how to make themselves better. Quetzalcoatl was happy because it seemed that *this* lot of people would survive.

As for the ants, they found that the people were much more useful to them now that they could feed themselves. The people began to cook and find new and delicious foods to eat, which the ants could also share.

How We Know

Have you ever wondered how, although the Aztecs lived over 400 years ago, we know so much about their daily lives?

Evidence from the Ground

The Spanish invaders razed Tenochtitlan to the ground, destroying most of the evidence of the Aztec way of life, but some Aztec artefacts remain. A few temples and cities were not pulled down and still stand today.

▲ It is amazing to think that the Aztecs who built this huge temple did not use wheels or metal tools.

Evidence from Books

The Spanish destroyed many Aztec books but some survived. One Spaniard, Bernardino de Sahagun, asked Aztec nobles to help him decipher Aztec books soon after the conquest. Other members of Cortes' invading forces wrote accounts of Aztec life in Tenochtitlan as it was before they destroyed it.

▲ Some Aztec codices have not yet been translated.

Evidence around Us

Descendants of the Aztecs still live in Mexico. Some of their daily customs date from Aztec times. Many still speak a form of the Aztec language, **Nahuatl**. Certain words of Nahuatl have passed into other languages, particularly those for types of food originally found only in Mexico, such as tomatoes (*tomatl*), chocolate (*chocolatl*) and avocados (*ahuacatl*).

Glossary

Anahuac
The name given by the Aztecs to the land they ruled.

barter
Buying and selling by exchanging goods rather than using money.

cacao
A type of bean used to make chocolate and cocoa.

calpolli
A small group made up of closely related Aztecs. (Aztec word)

causeway
A raised road or path across water.

chinampa
An island made from mud taken from the bottom of Lake Texcoco piled on top of plant material. (Aztec word)

codex (codices)
Name given to ancient manuscript volumes. Aztec codices are usually written on folded deerskin or bark paper.

digging stick
The only farming tool used by the Aztecs. A simple, long, straight stick used to dig trenches in the earth.

Great Speaker
The leader of the Aztecs. The Great Speaker was a nobleman who had usually been trained as a priest.

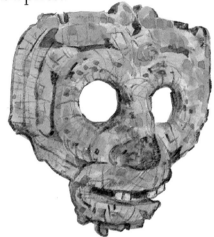

maguey plant
A plant with spiky leaves, part of the cactus family.

maxtli
Loincloth worn by Aztec men. (Aztec word)

pictogram
A symbol representing a word.

plateau
A large area of high, flat land.

pulque
An alcoholic drink made from the sap of the maguey plant.

pyramid
A building with sloping triangular sides. The Aztec pyramids were usually built as temples.

sacrifice
The killing of an animal or person as an offering to the gods.

Spanish Empire
In 1492 Ferdinand and Isabella of Spain sent Christopher Columbus on the journey that took him to America. For the next 100 years Spain spread its empire over most of South America and part of North America.

squash
A family of vegetables which includes marrows and gourds.

tlaxcalli
A flat corn pancake eaten with most Aztec food. Tlaxcallis are still eaten today, although they are usually known by the Spanish word tortilla. (Aztec word)

Index

For more information about TWO-CAN books, write to TWO-CAN Publishing, 346 Old Street, London EC1V 9NQ.